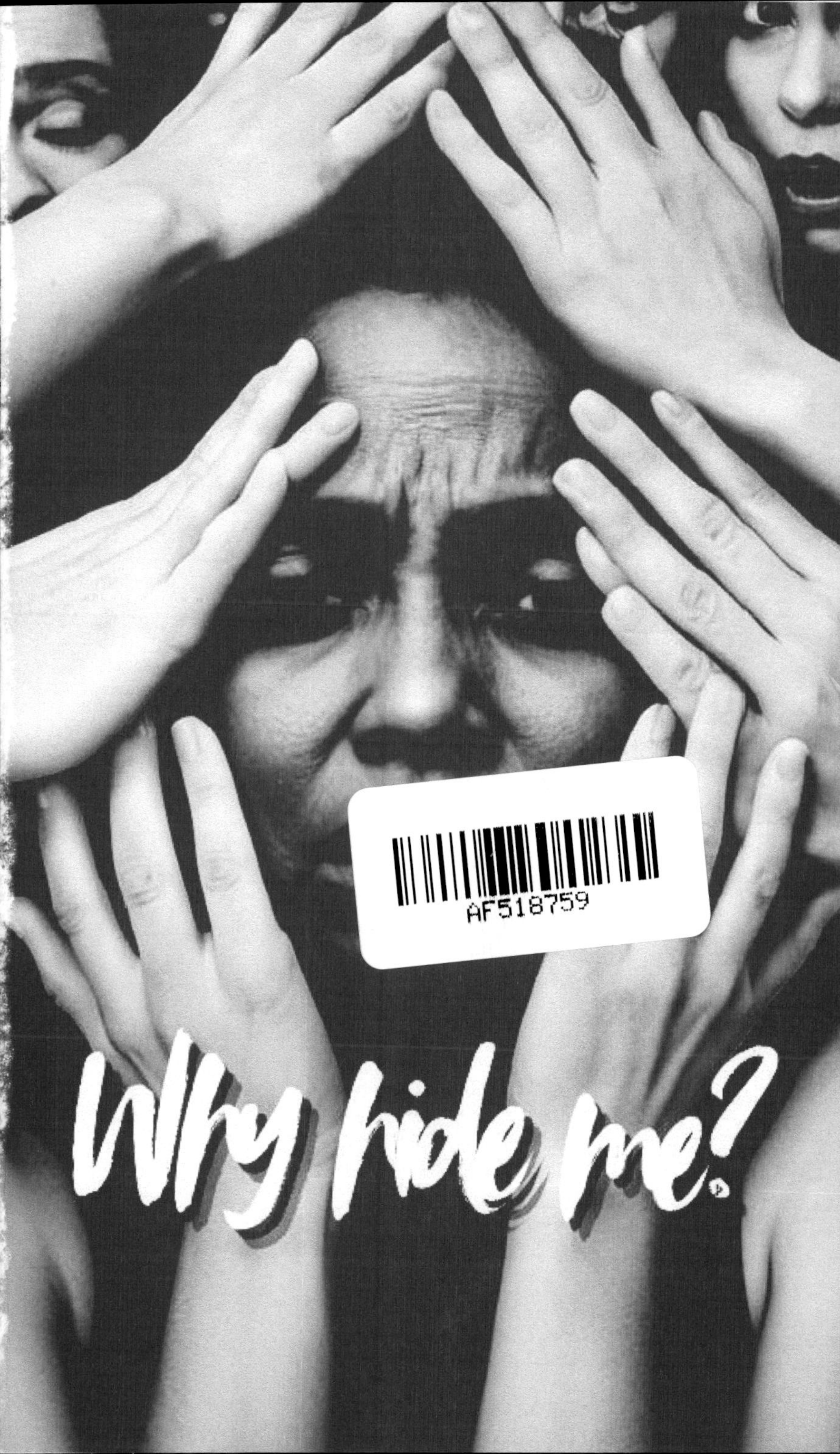
Why hide me?

BLUEROSE PUBLISHERS
India | U.K.

For permissions requests or inquiries regarding this publication, please contact:

BLUEROSE PUBLISHERS
www.BlueRoseONE.com
info@bluerosepublishers.com
+91 8882 898 898
+4407342408967

ISBN: 978-93-6783-707-8
EISBN: 978-93-6783-511-1

First Edition: February 2025

"My mental illness does not define who I am."

CRAZY
PITY
ILL
PITY
PITY
LINE
DENIAL

I can't be ill, Above all, mentally ill.
People will call me crazy,
Underestimate me, pity me.

Can't happen to me.
My karma list was clean.
I don't deserve even a bit
Of the horror it carries.

I don't need to be treated!
See, my health is perfectly okay.
No fever, no broken bones.
Why, then, am I declared mentally ill?

Being emotional—
How does that justify me being ill?
It's just the emotion that was spilled.
Not a big deal; I am not mentally ill.

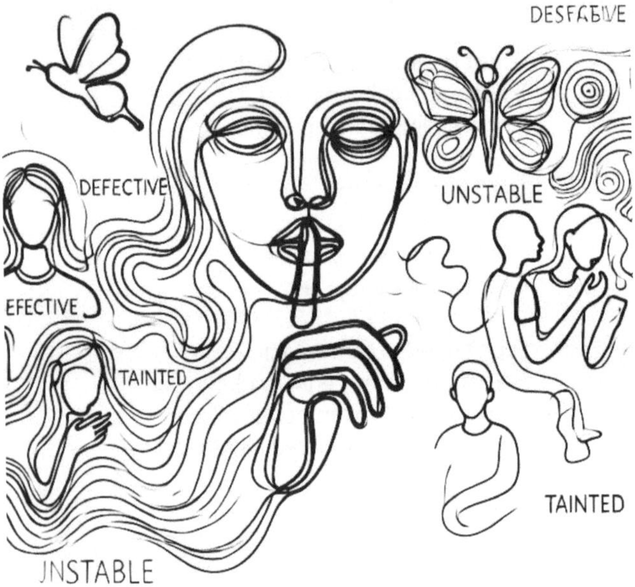
DEFECTIVE
UNSTABLE
EFECTIVE
TAINTED
TAINTED
NSTABLE

Sssshhh!!!
Someone might hear you,
What we all want buried.
Doomsday, if this shall surface.

No one would want to marry you,
Declared defective.
Used, like a secondhand phone.
This defect in you
Will attract deformities for you.

Even if someone sees you beyond it,
What will you bear?
A defective product results in an unstable relation
And a tainted child.

So, mum's the word.
When you meet him, just don't!
Don't show your colors.
Sssshhh!! Before the cat's out of the bag.

VULNERABITY
VULNERABLY
TRUTH
KEEP
SECRETS
TRUTH
TRUTH
TRUTH
TRUTH
TRUTH

How can I not?
Tell him the depth of my health.
Wouldn't it be cheating him,
Hiding something so crucial,
Crucial to check the susceptibility of this male? If
he is good enough to be engaged?

Does he deserve my eccentricities?
Is he suitable for the pages I fold?
Capable of resonating and keeping a hold?
Doesn't want to let go?

Cause at the end of the day,
Mr. To-Be-Wed will get to know
When he learns how I breathe.
Point it out,
And push me out of the door—
Is that what you want, Mom and Dad?

So, let's take a stand,
Show our cards.
Maybe he'll still want to trade his heart.

I have heard it all.
Called many names .
From my parents to my loved ones.
There is nothing new to me.
I'll give you a chance,
Why don't you give it a shot?
Pity me, look down on me,
Underestimate me.
Just because I'm mentally ill,
I can't perform on my behalf?
I need to be catered to?
Weak and timid, helpless?
Sleeping on my bed, covered in misery?

Honey, I might be in misery,
But I ain't helpless.
Fighting my battle with myself.
Time-consuming, sure,
But rest assured,
Fighters always do—always rise up.
Conquer the world
Because nothing scares them anymore,
Not even death standing at my door.

Acceptance
Perseverance
Support
Support

Are you ready?
Ready to accept?
Accept that I am mentally ill.
Will denial always be the face of it?
Come to this side, acceptance.
It's a blissful first step to perseverance.
Your daughter can't do it alone.
Hold my hand.
Let's walk through the door,
Vanquish our foes,
The battles in the walls within my head. Don't
be a hurdle for me,
For me to formulate a plan.
A plan to leave—
Leave you here and walk alone.
It's a long and rigid path,
To walk and run across the slope.
Mom, Dad, please don't make me,
Make me leave you,
Be all alone,
With a bully throned on my soul.

I don't know what could
Cause an outburst.
What's my trigger word?
Change my smile to enrage.
People around must live,
Live so scared, afraid—
Afraid of what next I might break.
Break to the point of rampage.

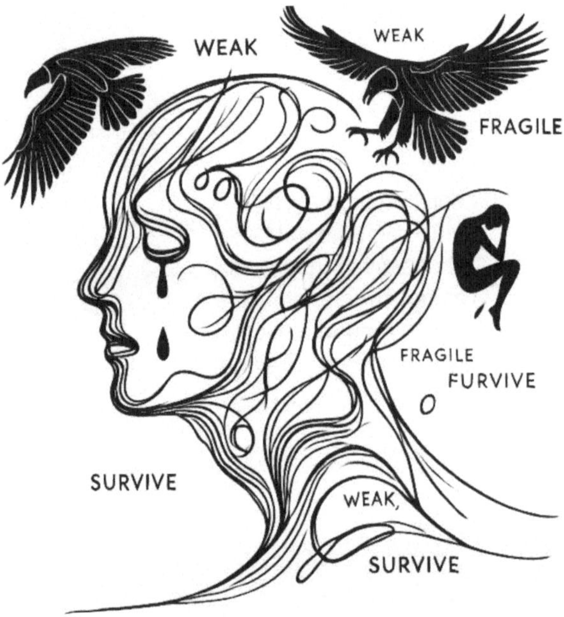
WEAK
WEAK
FRAGILE
FRAGILE
FURVIVE
O
SURVIVE
WEAK,
SURVIVE

You are too emotional.
Try not to cry every time in hardships.
You are fragile,
Too weak,
Too innocent.
You will be engulfed
By the vultures of the deemed.

It's not my wish to cry.
Tears just start rolling till my thighs.
If your voice even gets a decibel high,
I can't help it.
My emotions lashes with the other person's voice.
Can't help it, you say,
Maybe go hide and cry,
So that at least the truth is tucked inside.
Just be quiet if you want to survive.

CRY
WORTHY
WORTHY
WORTHY
ORTHY
FIGHT

Firstly, I'd like to stab him.
'Crying will not let you survive.'
Taking my basic right to cry.
Seemed too far-fetched,
Too emotional, really. Could I not survive?
Think again, is that right?
Or is it your insecurity Trying to subside
someone else's life?

Crying has so many biological upsides.
Have you ever counted?
Or just blabber with no knowledge in sight?
Crying is what makes a human.
If you don't like it, please move aside.
I'll cry, cry for everything
I feel worthy—
Worthy of a fight.

If it's a problem,
Then with a problem, you should die.

I wish I could shift the paradigm.
When my soul is ignites,
A craving subsides.
Its wait is my biggest enemy,
They call it's impulsivity.

It's true, it's hard to watch
The clock even hit a minute.
Patience is what I should have
Been told too many times.
I can't seem to understand what's wrong—
Letting your soul fill with its appetite.
Every time the sun is bright.

HIDE
SHAME
HIDE
DISFIGME
DISFIGURE

I hide, I hide
From anything that has a reflective side,
Far away from my eyes.
I can't find the courage
To look at my disfigured frame.
Is this a body?
You should be ashamed.
I know that's wrong to say,
But can't help it—
These are words embedded in my name.

I body shame my own self,
To a point where
The mirrors have been closed,
Closed for decades.

INSECURITY
INSECURITY - DOUBT
DOUBT
LOVE

The duration was a month
To believe he was attracted to me. Somehow
it seemed so fishy
That someone could also look at me,
With intentions of love.

For a month, I was in agony,
Thinking any minute he would laugh at me.
"Really? You thought I would be into you?
How funny is that?"
Even though we survived a year,
A doubt always reappeared.
Did he settle for me,
Or was it just my insecurity?

I couldn't keep track of my mood,
Swinging from one branch directly to the moon.
It was a normal Tuesday for me,
Until peers pointed out this weird thing in me.

CRASH
NUMB
NUMB

Crashes of feeling nothing
To feeling you are my world.
From your touch being orgasmic
To feeling like a dead body living.
My graph defies all the laws—
Laws for your safe keep,
For you to not be hurt,
Hurt by the hurricane to come.
Or maybe I am saving myself too.

delete
delete
run
run
break
break

I believed in a superpower I possessed—
To delete a person from my life with the drop of a hat.
Able to leave everything,
I loved, cared for my first love,
Because once, I felt not wanted.
(Well, he wanted to break up.)
Didn't try, literally not even once,
To suggest rekindling our first true love.
I ran, ran far away—
A wish I had not.

PATRENCE
EXTRENCE
PATIENCE
EXTRENCE
DISTANCE

Was told to take it slow,
Have patience,
Focus on the journey,
Stay on the grey.
But black and white is all I know,
Can't stay in between,
Can't either love or not.

You asked me of that,
Working away from the foundation.
To wait and put myself on hold,
Now look where we stand—
The same city, miles apart.
A lesson learned.

Cry
'Gobble
Explode
Cry
Gobble
Cry
Gobble
Explode
Explode

Even if I cried I consumed food,
Stomach aching, closing the door,
My mind wouldn't let the food go,
Munch it up till I overthrow.
I had to let that feeling go,
By eating it would subside within.
Gobble, gobble, like a pig—
Suits me perfectly, it was my star show.
Fat as fuck I was,
Still ate junk till I could explode.
Would cry, fight with my parents,
Break things, commit suicide—
Only if food was not by my side.

OVERTHINK
OVERTHINK
PATIENCE
PATIENCY
PATIENCE
SPACE

You couldn't say no to me.
You couldn't say I was a bad person.
You couldn't say "I love you" to me.
You couldn't say I did something wrong.
You couldn't say anything in a mad tone.
You couldn't say you want space from me.
You couldn't just question my beliefs.
You couldn't ask me to take the relationship slow.
You couldn't tell me to have patience.
You couldn't scold me.
You couldn't belittle me— I would overthink and maybe suicide.

TRUST
NO
TRUST
TRUST
TRUST
HURT

A "no" from my parents
Nearly almost killed my soul.
I hear, "I don't trust you,"
Hidden in the "no."

I couldn't fathom,
And hurt my vessel embodying my soul.
Bled myself a pool—
A pool of red rose.
Beautiful it seemed,
And made me happy to my core,
To see the damage it beholds,
To see the look on my parents' souls.
Look what you made me do.

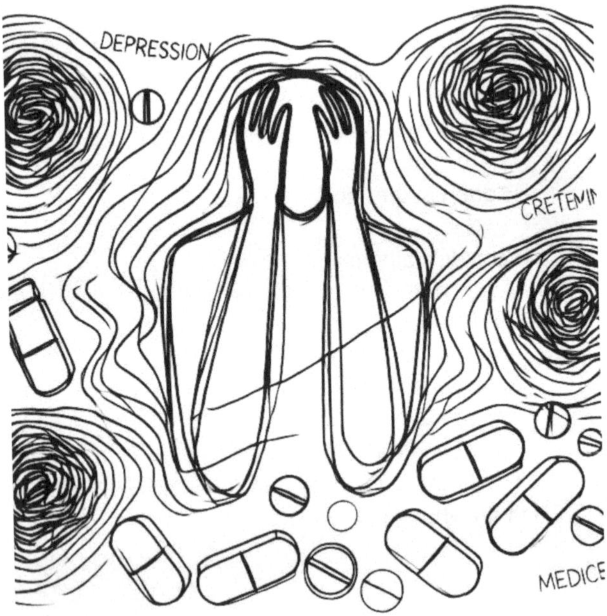
DEPRESSION
CRETEMIN
MEDICE

I didn't have meds for four nights.
Felt the wearing off tonight.
Depression creeping in,
Crawling to me,
Trying to approach my bright.

Mood swings from one planet to another,
Creeping in the terror.
Oh, what is in my medicine?

A journey existing just because of BPD.
Scratching my hair in agony.
Sleeping for hours in my bed,
Because it brings alongside depression and anxiety.
Crying, cutting, bleeding, working as pain relief.
Suicidal thoughts give me a sweet relief.
Repeated telecasts of, "It's okay, I can die,"
Kept me a bit sane at night.

Often then my body could survive,
I was awake all night,
My body sucked dry.
I just want to ask,
Can someone please pacify?

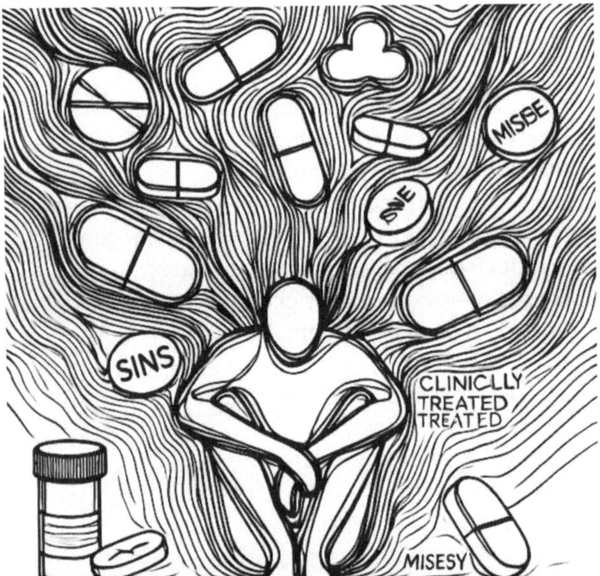
MISBE
SINS
CLINICLLY
TREATED
TREATED
MISESY

Who have I hurt in this oh-so-dreaded world?
I can't recall a single soul.
So why in the hell should I pay?
Pay for the sins I didn't create.

I didn't make me sick.
It was all their fault.
They troubled me, caused me misery, repercussions.
I'm dead from within.
Clinically treated.
Seven years ago.
Descends.

Every day a tablet.
To five of them.
Oh my god,
When will you end my misery?

N'T
WORTHY
MUSTN'T
MUSTN'Y
WORTHY
WOUTHY
DOUBT
DOUBT

I mustn't—
A tape recorder that won't shut up.
Every step I take reminds me
Of how to behave.
Behave in certain societal-defined lanes,
Crashed my self-esteem.
Like water clogged in streams.

I know many have tried,
Infiltrated my brain,
But the voice on my tape
Is the one person alone
Capable of destroying my strongest armed force.

"You mustn't," Mummy says.
Her comment alone changes the course—
Course of my game.

An outfit reflects
By just the turn of a phrase.
Impeccable it may be,
A doubt seems to appear:
Am I worthy,
Or should I disappear?

BURDEN
BURDEN
HURT
HURT
REALIZATION

Previously I believed it wasn't fair,
Was on a sinner's seat.
Who have I hurt?
Hurt to deserve this, not a soul I can recall.
So why should I carry this burden?

Perhaps there was one soul I didn't consider.
I am a human too,
Bullied and burned by yours truly.
So, you get it now?
Why are you dining on this table?

PERFECT
PERFECT
FEAR
PERFECT
FEAR
PERFECT
VULNERABLE
FEAR
VULNEABLE

Hooded by fear.
Unable to lift,
Lift even a single toe.
Worried that I can't be anything less,
Less than perfect.

So note down with me.
Can't scribble a mistake in notes.
Can't sit, unlike a lady.
Can't let anyone in.
Can't be vulnerable.

These are the don'ts.
If you want to survive,
Survive in this fear.
Listen to the mean voice in your head.

EXCUSED
CODING
EXCUSING
CODEG
CODING
TABU.ITY
SOCIAL MEDIA
CRAVE
CRAVE

Cloaked by my excuses,
On that was running my caravan.
I can't do this,
I can't do that.
It's out of syllabus—life.

Excuses, excuses, excuses.
I'm not saying I didn't try.
Multiple times, multiple careers,
Every failure I rose with another crave.
I wanna do teaching,

No, no, let's do coding,
Maybe Instagram—everything is out of shape.
I don't know how to maintain stability even for a day.

FEAR
AFFECTION
FEAR
AFFECTION
AFFECTION
DIRECTION
DIRECTION
AFFECTION

Have you ever felt the need
To cut the call before he does?
I don't know about you,
But that little thing is my fear of rejection,
Fear that has submerged—
Submerged my whole ecosystem,
Flinching from even a little affection.

Stay away.
My heart is under protection.
I can't feel left out, neither can I
Let him win.

In this made-up game of affection,
I can care less,
But still, am I in love?
Can anyone give me direction?

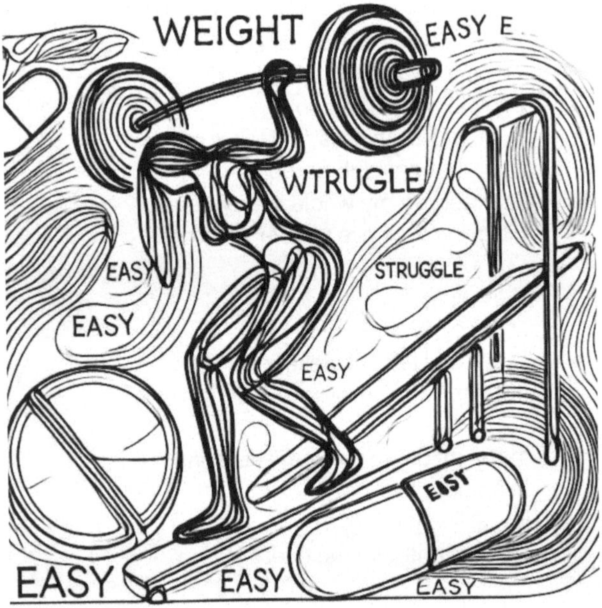
WEIGHT
EASY
WTRUGLE
EASY
STRUGGLE
EASY
EASY
EASY
EASY
EASY

It's too hard,
Even the thought of it—unfathomable.
I can't work out at all.
Lift a bone, run on a treadmill.
120 kg I hold.

How am I supposed to shed this unwanted mass,
Sweating and huffing?
By the thought alone,
Is there an easy way?
Maybe a pill I can take
For this to be easy,
A simple way?

TEARS
REALIZE
REALIZE
BREAK FREE

I hid under my depression.
Looked away from exertion.
This is not me.
I can't seem to soldier through.
Felt like bed was heaven.
And the world a cruel place to be.

The moment I realized
The severity of this lie,
Bed was entangling me,
Subsiding deep within the devil's eyes.
I woke up with tears in my eyes.

All these years I've wasted my life
Blaming the world, But didn't
realize I have been tearing myself,
Tearing with all my might. Thank
God in time I realized.

DEPRESSE
BLAME
REALIZE
HOME
R'OME
REALIZE

Don't get me wrong,
I did not choose depression,
Chose to be a victim,
Clueless of the solution,
Simmered in the problem for too long—
Too long to have consumed me,
Became like a home to me.

Well, how could I
Leave my home so easily?
For years counting seven,
Took me that long to know
That I could be fixed.
Blaming my depression—
"Others were to be blamed,"
My favorite obsession.

Thank God for the person who slapped,
Slapped some sense in me,
Or I would still be found
In my personal hell.

SNAP OUT
BLAME
OUT
BLAME
BEST
BAME
SNAP
OUT
PERSONNT HELL
BLAME
HELT

In the jail I built for myself,
Crippled by my mind on rollercoaster rides,
From growth to my demise,
Kept me occupied—
thank God for that guy,
Who slapped me,
slapped me for my welfare.

"Snap out of it," he said.
The comfort you seek from your bed—
Nothing but your personal hell.
Keep blaming the rest;
It isn't going to help you
To be your best.
"Snap out of it," he said.

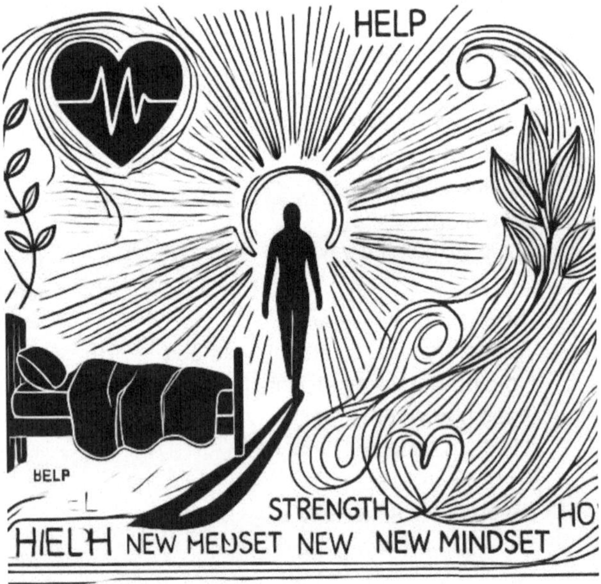
HELP
BELP
STRENGTH
HO
HIELH NEW MENSET NEW NEW MINDSET

It was that word he said—
"Your personal hell, your bed,"
Woke me up from this dream.

I don't need care, I need help,
Help that I can only commence.
Fully responsible, a mess,
Professional clinical help.

I left the past behind, at rest—
Most painful decision that day, that step.
Since then, every day a new fear, a new mindset.

LONELINESS
LONELINESS
ONELINESS
COST
COST
COST
LOVE

Oh my poor loneliness,
From one BF to another,
Just running from self.

Oh my poor loneliness,
From lie to self, And to
all others.

Oh my poor loneliness,
Please shower love,
begging to be pleased.

Oh my poor loneliness,
Feeling so sad for self,
Cut myself, attention.

Oh my poor loneliness,
So what did it cost
To not be alone?
Everything?

TRUST
TRAPS
PROTECT
TRUST — TRAPS - DESCEPTEN • PROTECT — PROTECT

I don't know when I am manipulated
To do the dirty work.
I didn't know how to identify those quirks.
Trusted each soul as if they were my own.

Slowly but steadily,
Learning the difference.
Identifying—
The cows, foxes, elephants.

Protecting it's my job From
the traps of these all.

ΓOLISH
WEAK
FOOLISH
WEAK
FOOLIS
WEAN
WEAK
WEAK
INFERIOR
INFERIOR
INFERIOR

I was protecting something,
Something eating from within.
My core beliefs,
Negative coping mechanisms I built.
To safeguard them,
Hefty prices to pay.
To be guarded, I choose to obey.

I am foolish,
I am small,
I am stupid,
I am weak,
I am inferior.

So tell me,
Why would I protect you?

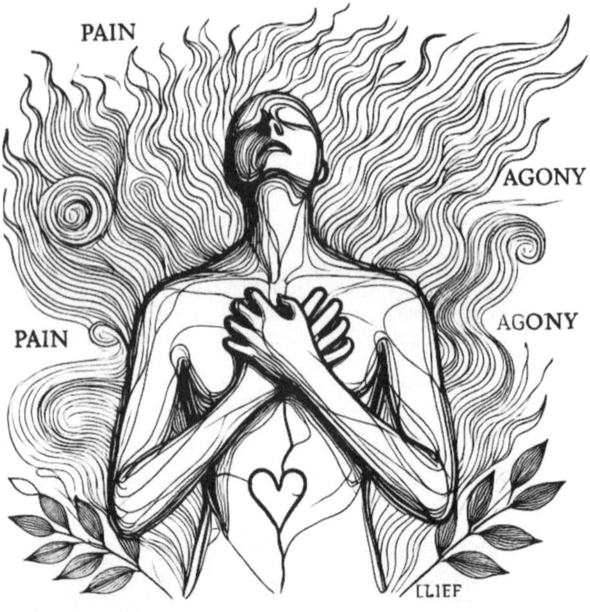
PAIN
AGONY
AGONY
PAIN

I feel like a cut on my wrist,
Where blood-rain flows,
Will do the job.
I will feel satisfied.

The pain is my relief.

There's agony in my heart.
It burns my soul.
To an extent, I wanna disintegrate to dust.

A cut saves me.
Harmful it may seem,
It does the job.

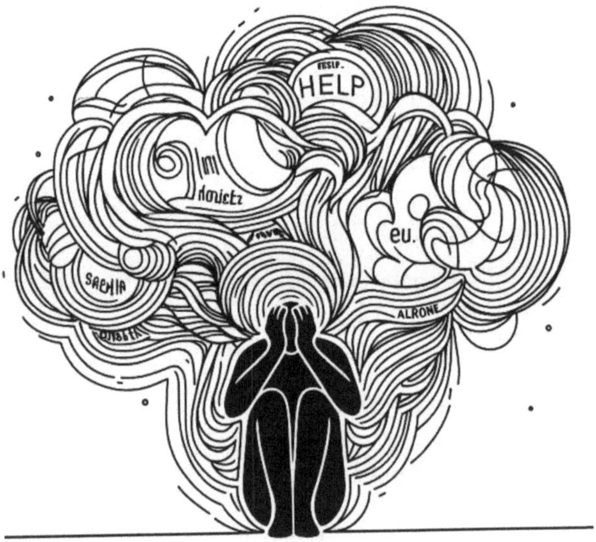
HELP
eu.
ALRONE

Well, again, here we are,
Feeling this again.
Wanna die? Cry.
Let me cut? Cry.
No medicine? Cry.

Now the people have started leaving me.
Taunting me:
"You can't be helped.
We tried our best.
You resent what's best.
Do these things,
Then we'll resume."

FREE WILL
INNOCENT
PROTECT
PROTECT

Innocent as claimed,
Gullible to even a child's play.
Can be fooled, you are a buffoon.
Don't take your own decisions,
Ingenious to their schemes,
You will regret if you don't listen.

Feeble-minded you seem,
Catastrophes keep entangling you,
Every new kite you release.

"Listen to your mummy papa,
Because fifty years of life they have lived.
Knows its nooks and crooks,
And I will protect you, baby.
Just release all your free will."

TAUNTINE
PILS
COURAGE
COURAGE
EXTARIDINARY
EXTARIDINARY

Why is it that I can't—
Can't eat my meds,
Can't be serious about such a big mess?

I gather courage,
Then again I seem to dispense.
I am telling you for certain,
It's my parents' fault,
And their taunting screws.

Their checking on me from time to time—
Is why I don't end up
Being the extraordinary self,
I always was meant to be.

HAUDE
FAULT
FIND
HIDE
FAULT
HIDE
FAULT
FAULT
FIULT
FIND
FAULT
FAULT
FAULT
FIND

I'll hide till no one can find,
So I'll do it by my might,
From all the errors in my life,
To finding pieces of art.

Living with my parents,
Back to square one—
Or is it the meds
I'm always in break from?
I can't be for sure.

Who am I kidding?
It's all my fault.

VALIIMATION
VALIIMATION
TRUST
NAGPUR
TRUST
ENOUGH
TRUST
ENOUGH
ENOUGH

Nagpur, next stop.
I don't understand why they don't trust.
Why is nothing ever enough?

May it be 100 copies I sell
Or 1000—it's never enough.
Why do I have this need?
The need to satisfy them.

By God, why?
Is there a need for me
To get their validation?
'Cause for every frown,
It kills me inside.

STRUGGLE
STRUGGLE
STRUGGLE
LIGHT
CONFLICE
CONFLICE

We know what's best for you.
Are you a 100% sure?

You, huh?
Alter personalities
Keep crowding my brain.
Day after day,
Keeps dominating, changing my ways.

My urge to do unethical.
Has overstayed.
I would say I have evil thoughts,
But who's to say
How long will it take
Until I am danger to me and others' way?

I wonder what it will take
To stick to normal norms of living,
And light up
When the sun shines on my face.

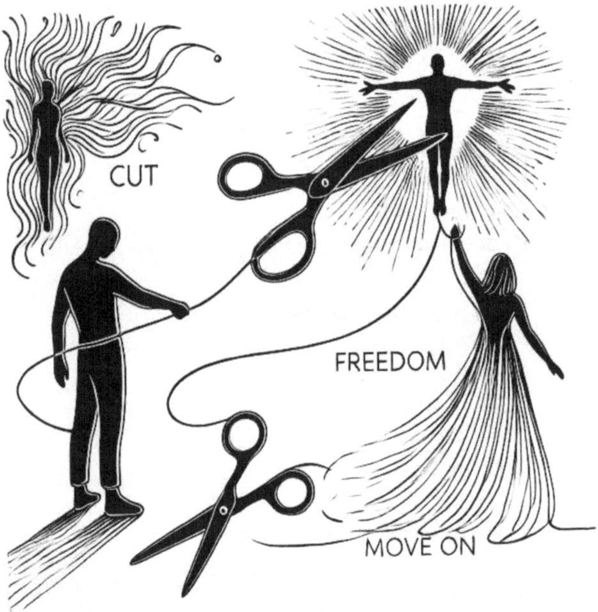
CUT
FREEDOM
MOVE ON

Whoever tells you,
"If you need their approval"

You don't trust them.
That's totally disastrous.

Run—
Run from the relationship you share.

TRIGGER
TRIGGER
CRAZY
SURVIVE
SURVIVE

Like a trailer of a horror movie—
Trigger alert: blood, cuts, and blades.
It's not easy living in my brain.

Supposedly, if you try,
How worse it is for me,
You won't even survive.

I live to brag these things,
I know it's crazy.
So don't peek in.

BALANCE
PAIN

Paralyzed.
Choose between happy and pain.
Happy is happy,
But pain keeps me alive.

The importance of life,
Which no matter how much I tried,
Felt numb in normal days.

Pain, once or twice a day,
Keeps happiness away.

REGRET
TRUST
#11
BESTSLER
REGRET
TRUST
DEUSTI
DECISIONS
#1 BESTSLER

For the first time,
#1 bestseller Amazon,
But seems like it wouldn't give me any gain,
As predicted.

Gullible, after all,
Took advantage of my innocence, trust.
The publication—I will not mention—
Seemed so fishy, now that I recall.

I must say, fine,
Can someone always take my decisions
From now onwards for me?

VALIDATION
VALIDATION
CONFIDENCE
PRETRETENDE
PRETEND
PRETEND

Now every decision,
Every step I take
Needs someone's validation
To ensure it won't be a mistake.

Self-decision?
What is that? I can't say.
My self-confidence has shattered.
Don't be mistaken—
I pretend like it's child's play.

An extrovert?
I guess that's my save.

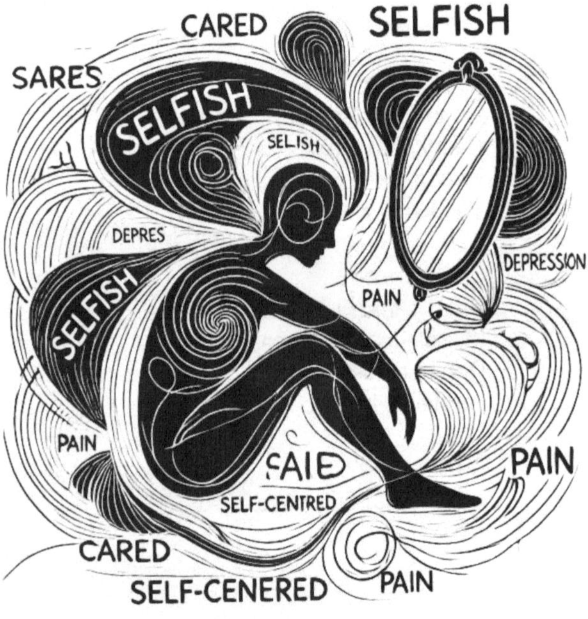
CARED
SELFISH
SARES
SELFISH
SELISH
DEPRES
DEPRESSION
SELFISH
PAIN
PAIN
PAIN
SELF-CENTRED
CARED
SELF-CENERED
PAIN

Selfish tags to my name.
"You never tend to others,
Just get your way."

Cry, "I have depression."
Introduce yourself:
"Hi, BPD is my name."

I sometimes doubt myself—
Am I not something other than
Just a self-centered mistake?

I believed, I cared.
Cared too much—that is pain.
But I guess,
Hollow are my claims.

ACCEPTANCE
TRUST
TRUST
HEALING

Key to cure is acceptance, they say.
I ain't denying in the first place.
I ain't running from my problems.

BPD is just a doctor's way
To scare and get me hooked on meds—
My initial thoughts.

But when I saw the change
In front of my eyes,
I cursed myself
For not trusting a professional's advice.

Now, happier than ever,
Two pills to pop a day.

HELP
CHALP
HELP
CHANGE
CHANGE
CHANGE

Didn't believe help I needed,
Resisted even the thought.

11th standard with no aims,
Sitting in front of the TV
With no education claims.

One day, *Modern Family*—
Alex was troubled, ahuh, lame.
Didn't hesitate.

Therapy ignited a spark.
If she didn't hesitate,
Why am I resisting?

A roadmap to health change.
Since that day, I don't budge.
Help—professional help—I take.

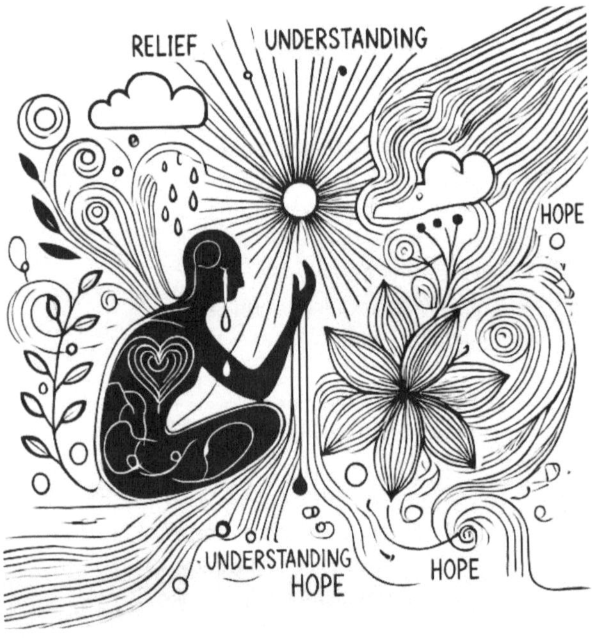
RELIEF
UNDERSTANDING
HOPE
UNDERSTANDING
HOPE
HOPE

A sense of relief, I must say.
In therapy, when I cry out my pain—
No fear of judgment,
When someone understands,
Someone explains why it pains this way.

You can't imagine the love,
The love it ignites again.
In your veins,
The world looks brighter again.

EMPATHY
CONNATHY
RELIEF

I remember the first time
I presented my case,
Explaining to a therapist
Why I behave this way.
Instead of what my parents would say,
This person understood,
Empathized with my tears,
Consoled me.
I have no words
To explain my feelings.
Someone found the reason
For my deranged way.

If You Need Help, Please Read This

If anything in this book feels familiar to you, even just a little, and you think you might need help, please don't hesitate to reach out. You don't have to face this alone.

The Rehabilitation Council of India (RCI) put together a list of certified clinical and rehabilitation psychologists. It includes professionals from all states and services in different languages, so you can find someone who understands you.

Here's the link:
https://rciregistration.nic.in/rehabcouncil/newsearchpage.jsp
I hope this helps you take the first step toward healing.